THE WORLD OF
DINOSAURS

LEVEL **2** READER

GRADES 1 TO 3

READING LEVEL

Written by Kathryn Knight
Contributing artist: Jeff Mangiat

bend⦿n

Dinosaurs

A dinosaur is an extinct animal in the scientific class of **Reptilia** (reptiles), but not all ancient reptiles were dinosaurs. True dinosaurs had limb joints that held the legs erect beneath the body, like bird legs. The legs of most reptiles splay out to the sides, like lizard legs. Some dinosaurs walked on four legs, but many walked upright on two, or switched back and forth. Dinosaurs shared their world with other amazing reptiles that walked the earth, swam in the sea, and soared through the air.

Brachiosaurus

Pronunciation: BRAK-ee-oh-SAWR-us
Name means: *Arm lizard*
Named by: Elmer S. Riggs, 1903
Family: Brachiosauridae
Lived: 153–113 million years ago
Areas found: Algeria, Portugal, Tanzania, USA (Colorado, Utah, Wyoming)
Height: 30–42 feet (9–12.8 m)
Length: 60–82 feet (18–25 m)
Weight: 45–55 tons*
Diet: conifers, cycads, ferns

Brachiosaurus was one of the largest land animals ever to have existed. This plant-eating giant had a long neck to reach treetops. It had a huge body, a long tail for balance, and a tiny brain.

*One ton is 2,000 pounds.

Dimetrodon

Pronunciation: die-**MET**-tro-don
Name means: *Two measures of teeth*
Named by: Edward Drinker Cope, 1878
Family: Sphenacodontidae
Lived: 280–245 million years ago
Areas found: USA, Canada
Height: 3 feet (0.9 m)
Length: 10 feet (3 m)
Weight: 400 pounds
Diet: other animals

Dimetrodon was not actually a dinosaur. It was a pelycosaur, a mammal/reptile-like creature that lived before the age of the dinosaurs. Its large sail was probably used to regulate body temperature.

Deinonychus

Pronunciation: dye-**NON**-ih-kus
Name means: *Terrible claw*
Named by: John Ostrom, 1969
Family: Dromaeosauridae
Lived: 115 million years ago
Areas found: USA (Montana, Wyoming, Oklahoma)
Height: 5 feet (1.5 m)
Length: 10 feet (3.5 m)
Weight: 175 pounds
Diet: dinosaurs and other animals

This dinosaur was built for speed! *Deinonychus* was a fearsome predator that hunted in a pack. It had excellent eyesight and sharp teeth. Its large hands swiped with 5-inch claws.

Archaeopteryx

Pronunciation: AR-kee-**OP**-ter-ix
Name means: *Ancient wing*
Named by: Christian Erich Hermann von Meyer, 1861
Family: Archaeopterygidae
Lived: 155–150 million years ago
Areas found: Germany
Height: 1 foot (0.3 m)
Length: 3 feet (0.9 m)
Weight: 2 pounds
Diet: insects

Dinosaurs looked like big reptiles, but in many ways they were built like birds. This feathered creature was a cross between a bird and a dinosaur. *Archaeopteryx* ate insects, which it caught in flight.

Megalosaurus

Pronunciation: MEG-uh-lo-**SAWR**-us
Name means: *Great lizard*
Named by: William Buckland, 1824
Family: Megalosauridae
Period: 181–169 million years ago
Areas found: Great Britain
Height: 12 feet (3.7 m)
Length: 30 feet (9.1 m)
Weight: 1 ton
Diet: other dinosaurs

Megalosaurus is famous for having been the first dinosaur to be scientifically described and named. It had a large head with very powerful teeth and a large powerful tail.

Utahraptor

Pronunciation: YOO-tah-**RAP**-tor
Name means: *Utah's predator*
Named by: Kirkland, Gaston & Burge, 1993
Family: Dromaeosauridae
Lived: 132–119 million years ago
Areas found: USA (Utah)
Height: 8 feet (2.4 m)
Length: 22 feet (6.6 m)
Weight: 1,500 pounds
Diet: other dinosaurs

Utahraptor was a fierce predator. It may have hunted in packs, bringing down large prey. Each back foot had a curved claw that could grow to 10 inches (25 cm) long! Scientists now believe that *Utahraptor* had feathers—but could not fly.

Baryonyx

Pronunciation: bare-ee-**ON**-ix
Name means: *Heavy claw*
Named by: Alan Charig & Angela Milner, 1986
Family: Baryonychidae
Lived: 120 million years ago
Areas found: Great Britain, Nigeria
Height: 6 feet (1.8 m)
Length: 35 feet (10.7 m)
Weight: 2½ tons
Diet: fish, carcasses
(dead animals)

The first *Baryonyx* bone was found in England in 1983. It is one of the few known piscivorous (fish-eating) dinosaurs. It had a long snout and narrow jaws, very similar to a crocodile's.

Carnotaurus

Pronunciation: KAHRN-uh-**TAWR**-us
Name means: *Flesh-eating bull*
Named by: José Bonaparte, 1985
Family: Abelisauridae
Lived: 97 million years ago
Areas found: Argentina
Height: 13 feet (4 m)
Length: 25 feet (7.5 m)
Weight: 1 ton
Diet: other dinosaurs

You would not want to meet
this guy in a world of dinosaurs.
Carnotaurus was a carnivore
(meat-eater) with a huge mouth
and sharp teeth. It had horns
and spikes down its
back. It probably
had tough, pebbly
skin like a reptile.

Pteranodon

Pronunciation: ter-**ON**-oh-don
Name means: *Winged toothless*
Named by: Othniel Charles Marsh, 1876
Family: Pteranodontidae
Lived: 89–70 million years ago
Areas found: USA
Length: 15–20 feet (4.5–6 m)
Wingspan: 20 feet (6 m)
Diet: fish

Pteranodon was not a dinosaur. It was a flying reptile. It had a toothless beak like a modern bird. It could soar through the air on the skin-flaps between its extra-long finger bones and body.

Velociraptor

Pronunciation: veh-**LOSS**-i-RAP-tor
Name means: *Swift thief*
Named by: Henry Fairfield Osborn, 1924
Family: Dromaeosauridae
Lived: 83–70 million years ago
Areas found: China, Mongolia
Height: 2½ feet (0.8 m)
Length with tail: 6 feet (1.8 m)
Weight: 33 pounds
Diet: other dinosaurs

Velociraptor was a quick, smart hunter! It was small—about the size of a turkey— with a long tail for balance. The sharp, curved claw on each foot was a deadly tool. *Velociraptor* probably had feathers but could not fly.

Allosaurus

Pronunciation: AL-uh-**SAWR**-us
Name means: *Other lizard*
Named by: Othniel Charles Marsh, 1877
Family: Allosauridae
Lived: 155–145 million years ago
Areas found: USA (Utah), possibly Portugal and Tanzania
Height: 17 feet (5.2 m)
Length: 35 feet (10.7 m)
Weight: 2 tons
Diet: other dinosaurs

Allosaurus was probably the most common carnosaur 150 million years ago. It was a large but speedy predator, running up to 20 mph. It had many sharp teeth and two horn-ridges on its head, one above each eye.

Plesiosaurus

Pronunciation: PLEH-see-oh-SAWR-us
Name means: *Almost lizard*
Named by: William Conybeare, 1821
Family: Plesiosauridae
Lived: 200–135 million years ago
Areas found: England, Germany
Length: 10–16 feet (3–5 m)
Weight: 1,000 pounds
Diet: fish, ancient
squidlike animals

Plesiosaurus was an aquatic reptile (not a dinosaur) that hunted in ancient seas with a mouth full of long, sharp teeth. *Plesiosaurus* did not move its paddle-like flippers front to back. It flapped them up and down, much like a penguin.

Tuojiangosaurus

Pronunciation: too-**HWANG**-oh-**SAWR**-us
Name means: *Tuo River lizard*
Named by: Dong, Li, Zhou, Zhang, 1977
Family: Stegosauridae
Lived: 156 million years ago
Areas found: China
Height: 11 feet (3.4 m)
Length: 23 feet (7 m)
Weight: 3 tons
Diet: low plants

Tuojiangosaurus had pointed bony back plates that may have served as protection as well as for temperature regulation.
Its long tail was a weapon—the sharp spikes could ward off most predators.

Ceratosaurus

Pronunciation: sih-RAT-uh-**SAWR**-us
Name means: *Horned lizard*
Named by: Othniel Charles Marsh, 1884
Family: Ceratosauridae
Lived: 156–144 million years ago
Areas found: USA, Tanzania
Height: 13 feet (4 m)
Length: 20–25 feet (6–7.5 m)
Weight: 1½ tons
Diet: other dinosaurs

This dinosaur had a large horn on its nose. Since *Ceratosaurus* was so large, the horn was probably not used for defense. It may have been a male characteristic. Or, as some scientists think, it may have helped hatchlings crack their way out of the shell.

Shonisaurus

Pronunciation: show-nih-**SAWR**-us
Name means: *Lizard from the Shoshone Mountains*
Named by: Charles Camp, 1976
Family: Shastasauridae
Lived: 216–203 million years ago
Areas found: USA (Nevada), Canada
Length: 50–70 feet
(15.2–21.3 m)
Weight: 25–30 tons
Diet: fish, marine animals

This huge creature looked like a dolphin, but it was a marine reptile—the largest that has yet been found. *Shonisaurus* was an ichthyosaur (fish-lizard), a fast-swimming predator that ruled the seas! *Shonisaurus* is the state fossil of Nevada, where so many bones have been found.

Pterodactylus

Pronunciation: TERR-oh-**DACK**-till-us
Name means: *Winged finger*
Named by: Jean Cuvier, 1809
Family: Pterodactylidae
Lived: 150 million years ago
Areas found: Europe, Africa
Height: 1 foot (0.3 m)
Wingspan: 3–5 feet (1–1.5 m)
Weight: 2–10 pounds
Diet: fish, small animals, insects

Pterodactylus was the first pterosaur to be named as a flying reptile (not a dinosaur). It soared on batlike wings, but was quadrupedal on land, walking on all four limbs.

Pachycephalosaurus

Pronunciation: pak-ee-SEF-uh-lo-SAWR-us
Name means: *Thick-headed lizard*
Named by: Barnum Brown and Erich Maren Schlaikjer, 1943
Family: Pachycephalosauridae
Lived: 68–65 million years ago
Areas found: USA (Montana, South Dakota, Wyoming)
Height: 10 feet (3 m)
Length: 16 feet (4.9 m)
Weight: 2 tons
Diet: plants, insects

Pachycephalosaurus walked on its two back legs. It had a 10-inch-thick domed skull, often adorned with "knobs" or spikes. It had a large sturdy body, short front legs, and a long, stiff tail.

Gallimimus

Pronunciation: gal-ih-MY-mus
Name means: *Chicken mimic*
Named by: Osmolska, Roniewcz & Barsbold, 1972
Family: Ornithomimidae
Lived: 73–65 million years ago
Areas found: Mongolia
Height: 11 feet (3.4 m)
Length: 20 feet (6 m)
Weight: 1,000 pounds
Diet: small vertebrates,
insects, plants

Gallimimus looked more like a large bird than a reptile. It had a long neck and toothless beak, similar to the ostrich of Africa and the emu of Australia.

Oviraptor

Pronunciation: oh-vih-**RAP**-tor
Name means: *Egg thief*
Named by: Henry Fairfield Osborn, 1924
Family: Oviraptoridae
Lived: 83–73 million years ago
Areas found: Mongolia
Height: 3 feet (0.9 m)
Length with tail: 6.5 feet (2 m)
Weight: 73 pounds
Diet: mollusks and shellfish

Once believed to have been an egg eater (hence its name), this dinosaur probably ate shellfish, which it crushed with its strong jaws and two small pointed teeth. It was very fast and looked similar to modern-day emus, rheas, and ostriches.

Archelon

Pronunciation: AR-chi-lone
Name means: *Ancient turtle*
Named by: G.R. Wieland, 1896
Family: Protostegidae
Lived: 70 million years ago
Areas found: USA (South Dakota, Kansas, Nebraska)
Length: 13½ feet (4 m)
Width: 16 feet (4.9 m)
Weight: 2½ tons
Diet: mollusks, squid

Archelon was not a dinosaur. It was the largest sea turtle that has ever lived—as big as a small car! It swam in shallow waters and probably had a lifespan of more than 100 years.

Struthiomimus

Pronunciation: STROOTH-ee-oh-**MY**-mus
Name means: *Ostrich mimic*
Named by: Henry Fairfield Osborn, 1916
Family: Ornithomimidae
Lived: 73–70 million years ago
Areas found: USA, Canada
Height: 7 feet (2.1 m)
Length: 13 feet (4 m)
Weight: 330 pounds
Diet: small animals, plants

This dinosaur was very
similar to the modern
ostrich (*struthio* in Latin).
It had small, drooping
arms, a long tail, and
dry scaly skin.
It could possibly run
up to 50 miles per hour.

READING
GRADES 1 TO 3
2
LEVEL

THE WORLD OF
DINOSAURS

Ancient Earth was alive with creatures that have long since died out. Discover these strange dinosaurs, and the flying, swimming, creeping reptiles that shared their world.

For Ages 6-9

Follow us for free activities, contests, crafts, and more!

f bendoninc   twitter bendon_inc   p bendoninc

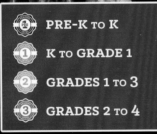

- PRE-K TO K
- 1 K TO GRADE 1
- 2 GRADES 1 TO 3
- 3 GRADES 2 TO 4

Distributed by Bendon, Inc. © 2017
Ashland, OH 44805
bendonpub.com   1-888-5-BENDON
Printed in Haining, Zhejiang, China
Bendon234251359F16818245-02/17

bendon

DPCI: 234-25-1359
ISBN 978-1-5050-9103-8

$1

9 781505 091038